Contents

About the authors

Kate Richardson is a highly specialist speech and language therapist working with adults with learning disabilities. She is a partner in Open Cultures research and training consultancy (www.openculturesconsultancy.com).

Rorie Fulton is a partner in Open Cultures. He also works as a mental health advocate and is co-ordinator of The Caldwell Autism Foundation, a charity supporting the communication needs of people who have autism (www.thecaldwellautismfoundation.org.uk).

Introduction

People with learning disabilities often depend on others for the support they need in order to live their lives. For this reason, effective communication is essential if people with learning disabilities are to secure rights, inclusion, choice and independence. The degree to which individuals depend on the support of others varies from one person to the next – support may be for just a couple of hours a week to do the shopping and make sure the bills get paid, or, for an individual with high support needs, it may be round-the-clock help from a small team of personal assistants. For all individuals, however, the effectiveness of the support provided depends on the quality of the relationship between the individual and those who support them. The quality of this relationship depends, in turn, on the quality of the communication between them.

Poor communication with people who have learning disabilities has consequences that range from the relatively insignificant – an individual is taken to the shops when they would prefer a walk in the park – to the catastrophic. The failure of public services to make reasonable adjustments regarding communication not only makes it extremely difficult for people with learning disabilities to access services, but it may also breach the Equality Act (2010) and Article 8 of the European Convention on Human Rights (Michael, 2008, p24).

Throughout this guide there are a number of thinking activities that will help further your understanding of the issues as well as some practice activities that will require you to complete answers in the book.

In light of the above, this guide adopts an explicitly rights-based approach to communication. Such an approach is founded on the assertion that everyone has a right to communicate effectively in order to work towards and develop the life they want for themselves. It also recognises that not everyone is equally able to communicate effectively and that certain groups in society face barriers when communicating. A rights-based approach therefore uses a 'human rights lens' to look at these barriers.

Human rights are rights that belong to everyone. They are the basic rights each of us has simply because we are human – no matter who we are, where we live or what we do. Human rights aim to protect all that is important to us as human beings, such as living our lives the way we want to and being treated with dignity and respect. Human rights are not for the protection of a particular group or groups in society – they provide a practical framework to protect the rights of everyone. However, while human rights apply equally to all citizens, they are especially important for people with learning disabilities because such individuals often have communication needs and require support from others to live their lives. A rights-based approach to communication can support people with learning disabilities to enjoy and experience the benefits of effective communication in their daily lives.

Who might benefit from this guide?

A wide range of practitioners could benefit from this guide, including:

- personal assistants
- support workers
- learning disability service providers
- advocates
- self-advocates
- family carers
- frontline public service workers (such as midwives, health visitors, social workers, family centre staff, family support workers, job centre employees and police officers)
- nurses (acute and community)
- GPs
- GP receptionists
- occupational therapists
- psychologists
- psychiatrists
- positive behaviour support practitioners
- physiotherapists
- counsellors
- volunteers working in the learning disabilities sector
- legal representatives
- court-appointed guardians.

A word about Total Communication

It is important to remember that Total Communication is an approach to communication, not a specific set of techniques that must be followed in a particular way. Rather, it encourages the use of a range of different communication techniques in addition to the spoken word, depending on the communication skills and the needs of the individual in question.

'Total Communication means using different ways of communicating according to each situation and person.' (Oxfordshire Total Communication, 2012)

Section 4 of this guide, A Total Communication approach, therefore provides a brief introduction to a number of different communication techniques. You can then go away and find out more about those techniques that might enhance your communication with the individuals you support. As such, Section 4 aims to provide no more than a taster of the different communication techniques in the hope that you will then be inspired to go and find out more.

Links to other qualifications

This guide covers:

- **QCF unit SHC 021:** Introduction to communication in health, social care or children's and young people's settings (three of the four learning outcomes)

- **QCF unit LD 201:** Understand the context of supporting individuals with learning disabilities, learning outcome 6: Know how to promote communication with individuals with learning disabilities (core unit for both levels 2 and 3)
- **Standard 3** (Communicate Effectively) of the refreshed Common Induction Standards (three of the four learning outcomes)
- **Standard 2.2** (Communicating in an appropriate, open, accurate and straightforward way) of the General Social Care Council Code of Practice for Social Care Workers
- **Principle 2** (Communicate effectively to enable individuals to assess their needs, and develop and gain confidence to self care) of Skills for Care's Common Core Principles to Support Self Care.

In addition, the guide relates to other national occupational standards and professional standards, including:

- National Occupational Standards for Health and Social Care, throughout which the theme of communication recurs
- National Occupational Standards in Children's Care, Learning and Development unit CCLD 201 Contribute to positive relationships
- the performance criteria of Workforce Competence GEN22 Communicate effectively with individuals
- NHS Knowledge and Skills Framework Dimension: Core 1 Communication Level 2: Communicate with a range of people on a range of matters.

References

Michael J (2008) *Healthcare for All: Report of the independent inquiry into access to healthcare for people with learning disabilities* [online]. Available at: http://webarchive.nationalarchives.gov.uk/20130107105354/http://www.dh.gov.uk/prod_consum_dh/groups/dh_digitalassets/@dh/@en/documents/digitalasset/dh_106126.pdf (accessed March 2015).

Oxfordshire Total Communication (2012) *What is Total Communication?* [online]. Available at: http://www.oxtc.co.uk/contact.shtml (accessed January 2015)

Communication: the basics

Introduction

This section aims to explore what is meant by the term 'communication', to help you think more deeply about communication and what it might mean in the context of supporting people with learning disabilities. It looks at how we communicate and the reasons why we do so, both in the context of supporting people with learning disabilities and more generally in our day-to-day lives.

What is communication?

Communication is a basic human activity, but there are many different ways of defining it.

It is a two-way activity, involving understanding as well as expression. It is a process by which information is both expressed and understood by those communicating. It is a shared activity in which one person 'sends' a message and the other person 'receives' it and responds accordingly.

Communication requires a shared language, but this does not necessarily mean a spoken language – it might be sign language for people with hearing impairments, for example, or another visual 'language' for people who are non-verbal. In order for any communication to take place it is vital to establish the language/s that work best for person you are supporting. Importantly, communication, be it intentional or otherwise, is a point of connection – a meeting of two human beings and it is central to our ability to take our place as valued members of society (Thurman, 2009).

How do we communicate?

People communicate in all sorts of ways in their everyday lives. As well as verbal communication, we also use a variety of non-verbal communication methods. Remember, all the different

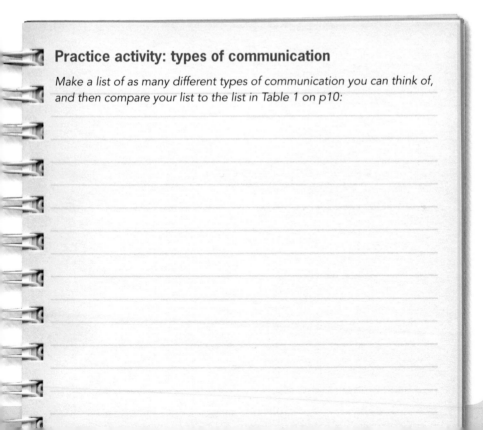

Practice activity: types of communication

Make a list of as many different types of communication you can think of, and then compare your list to the list in Table 1 on p10:

ways of communicating – non-verbal as well as verbal – are equally valid and meaningful.

There is, for example, some well-known research (Mehrabian, 1971) that suggests that only seven per cent of communication is verbal and the remaining 93% is communicated by body language, facial expression, tone and so on. How you say something is therefore just as important as what you say, and often more so.

Thinking activity

What kinds of communication – whether verbal or non-verbal – might people with learning disabilities rely on? What implications does this have for the way you communicate with the person or people you support?

Table 1: Methods of communication

- speech/talking
- facial expression (eg. frowning to show that you don't understand)
- gestures (eg. finger wagging to tell a child off)
- body language (eg. crossing your arms or turning your back)
- informal signing (eg. signing for a drink in a pub)
- writing (eg. letters, texts or emails)
- pictures (eg. instructions on flat-pack furniture)
- symbols (eg. road signs or icons on your mobile phone)
- objects of reference (eg. shaking your car keys to say 'shall we go now?').

This is not a comprehensive list, other forms of communication will be introduced in subsequent sections.

In the context of supporting people with learning disabilities, effective communication can only take place when we see the individual as worthy of being communicated with, and when we remember that, despite the challenges sometimes faced, effective communication is just as achievable with that individual as it is with anyone else.

Communication is collaborative – how much you, as the individual's communication partner, are called upon to contribute depends on whom you are talking to, for example, a baby, a child, a person who speaks a different language, an individual with learning disabilities or an individual with a hearing impairment. Different individuals have different communication needs and so will require from you different levels and types of collaboration.

Effective communication is therefore the product of a partnership for which you, as the individual's communication partner, are primarily responsible.

Why do we communicate?

People communicate with each other for a wide variety of reasons, including:

- to ask for things
- to express preferences and make choices
- to say 'yes' or 'no'
- to communicate experiences
- to communicate feelings and emotions
- to have a say
- to make services responsive to our needs
- to express an opinion
- to get something off our chest
- to express who we are
- to feel valued and listened to
- to have control over our life
- to be independent
- to build and sustain relationships
- to develop social networks
- to help others to feel included.

For all of us, communication serves not just 'to get things done', it is also about building meaningful relationships with the people around us. Our social and emotional well-being is developed and nurtured through these communicative interactions.

Practice activity: social and functional communication

Record in the columns below which of the reasons for communicating listed above are social or emotional, and which are task-related

Social or emotional	Task-related

Thinking activity

Think of the daily communication that you have with the individuals you support. What proportion of your communication with them would you say is functional and what proportion is social/emotional?

Next, think of the daily communication that you have with your friends and family. What proportion of this communication is functional and what proportion is social/emotional?

We can therefore say that any communicative interaction aims to meet either social/emotional needs (eg. to feel included or to have a say) or functional/task-related needs (eg. to get the individual to make a plan or to achieve a specific outcome).

References

Thurman S (2009) *Communication is a Human Right.* Kidderminster: British Institute of Learning Disabilities.

Mehrabian A (1971) *Silent Messages: Implicit communication of emotions and attitudes.* Belmont, CA:Wadsworth Publishing Company.

The communication jigsaw

Introduction

This section aims to provide you with a deeper understanding of the interlocking elements of good communication. It introduces the EPIC model of communication (Fulton & Richardson, 2012) and explores factors such as the communication environment, the communication partner, the individual's communication skills and the communication culture within which the interaction is taking place.

The EPIC model of communication

A jigsaw is a good metaphor for thinking about communication because it conveys in quite simple terms the idea that, for good communication to happen, certain elements must first be in place. When we think of communication as a jigsaw, it becomes clear that good communication cannot take place until and unless all the pieces of the jigsaw are present and fit together properly.

The communication jigsaw has four interlocking elements and together these make up the EPIC model of communication:

- E – the communication **E**nvironment
- P – the communication **P**artner
- I – the **I**ndividual's communication skills
- C – the communication **C**ulture.

Imagine these four elements as pieces of a jigsaw, as in Diagram 1.

The communication partner is the key element at the centre of the jigsaw with which the other elements interlock. As you read through the rest of this section, think about why the key element is the communication partner rather than any of the other elements.

Diagram 1: the communication jigsaw

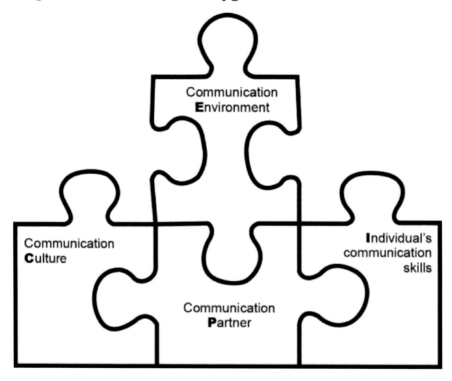

The communication ENVIRONMENT

The communication environment is the location where communication takes place, but it also includes the ways in which communication is supported or made difficult in that place.

Consider, for example, the places where you enjoy effective communication with your friends, family or work colleagues, such as driving in a car (no distractions, side-by-side and one-to-one), at the pub (relaxed but a lively atmosphere), going for a walk (fresh air and solitude) or in a meeting room (privacy and quiet, away from a busy office floor).

Now compare these with places where you might find it difficult to communicate, for example in a noisy

Thinking activity

Think of your own work setting. To what extent do you feel that the communication environment supports good communication? Or does the environment make communication difficult for individuals with learning disabilities?

staff room where there is little privacy, in a busy restaurant or at home when the TV and radio are on at the same time.

Different people communicate better in different environments, and this is equally true for individuals with learning disabilities. For effective communication to take place between you and the person you are

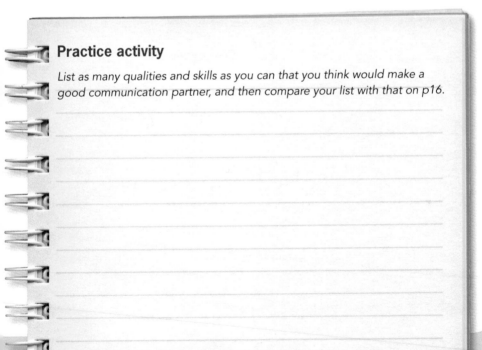

Practice activity

List as many qualities and skills as you can that you think would make a good communication partner, and then compare your list with that on p16.

supporting, it is therefore essential that you know about the different ingredients that make up their preferred communication environment (eg. low lighting, no distractions, sitting comfortably) and ensure to the best of your abilities that these are in place when you communicate with the person.

The communication PARTNER

The communication partner is the most important element in the EPIC model of communication. The role of the communication partner is fundamental not only to effective individual acts of communication, but also to inclusion and access to richer life experiences for people with learning disabilities.

Essential to being an effective communication partner is the

desire to communicate – if you are distracted and not giving your full attention to the person you are supporting, then effective communication cannot take place.

The qualities and skills that make a good communication partner include:

- a genuine desire to be with the person
- a good understanding of the person's preferred communication environments
- a good understanding of the person's communication skills and abilities
- empathy
- active listening skills
- attentiveness to the person's invitations to communicate
- patience
- effective use of facial expression
- good use of eye contact
- politeness and respect
- speaking slowly and clearly
- avoiding jargon
- lack of self-consciousness
- a knowledge of signing eg. Makaton
- talking about things the other person wants to talk about
- good teamworking skills.

The INDIVIDUAL'S communication skills

The individual's communication skills are the third element of the jigsaw. People with learning disabilities have a wide range of communication skills and abilities and it is important to remember

Examples:

Alison is non-verbal but is still able to dictate her environment through gesture. She likes a lot of sunlight but shuts the blinds at dusk. She doesn't mind some background noise when she's out, such as in a busy café, as long as her communication partner is close to her and can give her eye contact. It is important that only one person communicates with her at a time otherwise she struggles.

Peter has pictures around him so he can communicate through pointing.

that all ways of communicating are equally valid. It is essential that you to get to know the person's communication abilities and preferences, and your observation skills are a key part of this process.

When supporting a person with learning disabilities who uses verbal communication, you need to have a good knowledge of their communication skills, both receptive and expressive, so that you can adjust your spoken communication accordingly. This means, for example, avoiding the use of jargon and long, complicated sentences. As a communication partner, you should always supplement your spoken communication with other means of communication to make your meaning clear. For example, you might use pictures, facial expression, objects of reference or eye contact and so on.

People with learning disabilities who lack verbal skills may use a range of other approaches to communication, including:

- signing
- pictures
- pointing
- eye gaze
- communication passports
- gesture
- objects of reference
- facial expressions
- vocalisation
- touch
- patterns of sounds
- body language
- stereotyped movements

Thinking activity

Think of an individual you support. Can you list the various communication skills they have? Are there any means of communicating that they find difficult?

- devices such as talk boards, iPads or laptop computers.

The communication CULTURE

The communication culture of a setting is the final element in the jigsaw. Every organisation has its own communication culture which influences how the people who work there interact with each other and respond to events.

Some communication cultures will proactively support effective communication, others might need to be modified.

A positive communication culture:

- Places a high value on good communication.
- Views communication as the key to building relationships between people.
- Supports staff and managers to know and understand the communication skills of all service users.
- Supports staff and managers to know each service user as an individual and so be able to communicate with them effectively.

Practice activity

Read the following statements and put a tick or cross beside each depending on whether or not you agree with it.

1. There is no such thing as a positive or negative communication culture – communication just happens.

2. At the end of the day, either a service user can communicate or they can't, so for people with learning disabilities a positive communication culture is neither here nor there.

3. Communication is something quite straightforward and uncomplicated. It is about exchanging information and getting the job done.

4. A manager (or parent, head teacher or chief executive) cannot influence or change the way communication takes place in the setting for which they are responsible – the people in that setting simply communicate in the way they communicate.

5. A positive communication culture is the result of staff and management working together for the benefit of the service users.

6. Getting a buzz out of communicating with someone is only possible with people you know really well.

7. A positive communication culture is about how staff and managers communicate with service users. It has nothing to do with how managers and staff communicate with each other.

8. A positive communication culture means never feeling uncomfortable when you are communicating with a service user.

9. A positive communication culture means trying anything in order to communicate. After all, that is what people with learning disabilities have to do.

10. Communication is about taking risks.

- Encourages and enables staff and managers to reflect on and develop their own communication skills as well as those of the people they support.
- Encourages and enables staff and managers to try anything when it comes to finding ways of communicating with service users.
- Is always open and evolving.

Changing the communication culture

Changing the culture where you work is never easy, especially if you are not the manager. It can be done though, it just takes time. Modelling good practice is central to changing the communication culture of an organisation. If you work in a way that values and respects communication, this will inspire others to follow suit.

A communication culture can be modified by:
- modelling good practice
- championing the importance of good communication
- raising awareness
- celebrating success (however apparently small!)
- challenging poor practice in a supportive and constructive manner.

And when can a communication culture be modified? Any time! But especially:
- during everyday interactions with clients, colleagues and managers
- during team meetings
- during supervision
- during annual reviews.

The key role of the communication partner

Of the four elements that together make up the EPIC model of communication, the key element that links all the others together is you, the communication partner.

The reason for this is that the communication partner:
- is able to identify the individual's unique communication skills and support the individual to develop them
- can get to know the individual and the different factors that may affect their communication (eg. fatigue, health status, effects of medication, mood, recent events or behaviour triggers)
- can get to know and interpret the individual's non-verbal communication (eg. behaviour, posture, engagement/withdrawal and appetite)
- is able to modify and develop their own communication skills
- is able to modify the communication environment to make the most of the individual's communication skills
- is able to modify the communication culture to make the most of the individual's communication skills.

Reference

Fulton R & Richardson K (2012) *Effective Communication with People with Learning Disabilities*. Brighton: Pavilion Publishing and Media.

Section 3
Communication repair

Introduction

This section sets out strategies for repairing communication when it breaks down, as well as for avoiding or reducing the chances of communication breaking down in the first place.

Strategies for repairing communication

The consequences of communication breakdown for people with learning disabilities can range from mildly annoying to catastrophic. Many, if not most, instances of communication breakdown can either be avoided entirely or else managed by the use of effective repair strategies.

It is the support worker who will need to manage and, ideally, repair a breakdown in communication rather than the individual with a learning disability. There are a variety of strategies that a support worker can use in these situations.

For example, if you are struggling to communicate with someone with learning disabilities:

- Think about the bigger picture of the person's life – think about what they have done recently, where they have been, who they have been with.

- Ask the person about different topics – is it to do with the day centre? Is it about your key worker?

- Try asking 'can you show me?'

If the person is finding it hard to understand you, then repeat what you are saying, try saying it another way, give them time to process what you are saying or use visual supports such as sign or symbols. If the person is non-verbal, you may need to:

- use an object of reference

- use a picture

- check the time – is there something

Thinking activity

What strategies do you use when communication breaks down between you and a partner, friend or family member? Do you, or could you, use any of these in your role as a support worker?

that's usually done at this time of day that has been forgotten?

- reflect – have you seen this behaviour before?

At all times, be prepared to try anything!

It is important that you do not neglect any resources or people around you who may be able to help, and you shouldn't be afraid to ask for help if you need it. It's better to admit that you don't know and get help than to just ignore a breakdown in communication. Ignoring a breakdown in communication can leave your communication partner feeling despondent, not listened to and not valued, with the result that, in time, they may give up on communicating with you.

Remember:

- You will not be with the individual all the time, so maybe a colleague has seen a particular behaviour, gesture or sign before and knows what it means.

- It may be something that has been taught in a day centre, at college or at home.

- You may need to ask family

members or friends if they have seen the behaviour, gesture or sign before.

You therefore need to rely on your colleagues and the individual's family and friends and also always remember to share information you discover yourself as this may help a colleague who is struggling to communicate with the individual. It is also important to remember that a person's communication may differ depending on whom they are communicating with.

Don't forget, it is okay to say 'shall we take a break and try again later?', as long as you make sure you remember to try again.

Strategies for avoiding communication breakdown

While the above will help you if communication breaks down between you and someone you support, ideally this breakdown should be avoided in the first place. While this may not always be possible, very often there are strategies you can use that will prevent communication from breaking down.

An individual's communication skills can deteriorate over a short space of time for no apparent reason. An individual's behaviour may similarly alter for no apparent reason, to the extent that it becomes challenging to staff.

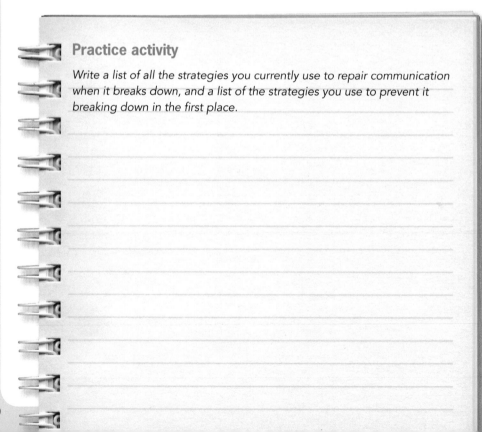

Practice activity

Write a list of all the strategies you currently use to repair communication when it breaks down, and a list of the strategies you use to prevent it breaking down in the first place.

Case studies:

Jason got very depressed for no apparent reason until the optometrist discovered he had cataracts. His surgery was successful and Jason's behaviour improved to the point where his mother said he 'was his old self again'.

Douglas's red eyes were the result of glaucoma, not hay fever as his sister had thought. Urgent treatment saved his sight.

(DOCET, 2000)

Possible reasons for such changes might include:

- recent experiences in the individual's life (eg. bereavement, moving home, change in primary carer or the end of a relationship)
- behaviour triggers (eg. previous experience of care and support, whether in a family or institutional context; experience of abuse)
- unidentified pain owing to diagnostic overshadowing (when a person's presenting symptoms are put down to their learning disability rather than another potentially treatable cause being sought such as mental ill-health)
- unidentified pain or ill-health owing to missed or overdue health checks
- unidentified pain or discomfort owing to missed or overdue dental checks
- temporary sensory impairment owing to missed or overdue sight or hearing tests.

There are two default strategies that support workers should therefore use in order to avoid communication breakdown:

1. Know the individual you are supporting well – know their past as well as their recent and ongoing experiences. Speaking to colleagues and family members should be part of the process of getting to know the individual.

2. Support the individual to have all the health checks that they need and to which they are entitled.

Reference

Docet (2000) *Making a Difference: Professional eye care for people with learning disability* [online]. Available at: http://www.docet.info/filemanager/root/site_assets/making_a_difference_module_1.pdf (accessed November 2014))

A Total Communication approach

Introduction

This section provides an introduction to using a Total Communication approach to support people with learning disabilities to enjoy good communication with the people around them. It will introduce you to the core concepts underpinning the approach and then give a brief overview of some of the techniques that can be used.

Introduction to Total Communication

The Total Communication techniques outlined in this section do not represent a definitive list and it is beyond the scope of this guide to give advice on putting the techniques into practice with individuals. Expert advice should be sought from the speech and language therapist of your local learning disabilities service (For information on how to find a speech and language therapist, see: http://www.rcslt.org/speech_and_language_therapy/how_to_find_an_slt/howtofind).

What is Total Communication?

Total Communication is something we can add to the spoken word that really helps people to connect. It is anything we can come up with that can help us to be with a person in a more supportive, useful and rich way.

The techniques explored in this section are:

- simplifying speech
- listening to facial expressions, body language and behaviour
- eye gaze
- gesture
- objects for communication
- signing
- pictures, photographs and symbols
- communication passports and multimedia profiles
- visual timetables
- hi-tech communication aids.

Thinking activity

Think of different aspects of your spoken communication that you may need to monitor and modify when speaking to someone who has a learning disability.

The techniques
Simplifying speech

When we are being given information, we all find it easier when people speak clearly and to the point. That way, there is less to understand and less to remember. When you are using verbal communication with someone who has a learning disability, it is especially important that you monitor your own speech to make sure you are speaking clearly and to the point.

Remember the EPIC model of communication – when you are thinking about modifying your spoken communication, always consider:

- the impact of the communication environment (eg. can the individual hear you properly? Can they see you properly? Does the environment promote effective communication or are there lots of distractions?)
- the different ways you could modify your spoken communication
- the individual's spoken communication skills

Practice activity

Match each of the ten statements in the left-hand column with the corresponding statement on the right. To do this, write the relevant number from column A in the appropriate box in column B.

A			B
1	Break information down into manageable chunks	Say 'the party starts at seven o'clock' instead of 'the party starts when everyone gets here after they've finished work'	
2	Try to avoid abstract language, which is difficult to understand	Be sure to maintain eye contact when you are communicating with the person you are supporting	
3	People with learning disabilities often need time to process what is being said to them	Say 'the towels go in the cupboard' instead of 'don't put the towels on the table'	
4	Sometimes a situation means that you have to use a negative to a person who does not understand negatives	Say 'my husband made the cake' instead of 'the cake was made by my husband'	
5	Do not use jargon	If the person describes themselves as feeling 'upset' or 'cross' when they are angry, use 'upset' or 'cross', not 'angry'	
6	When communicating, eye contact can be important for people with learning disabilities	Say 'the bus is late' instead of 'the bus is unexpectedly delayed'	
7	Time concepts can be difficult for some individuals to understand	Say 'we're going to the bank. After that we're going to the café' instead of 'we'll go to the café later but first let's go to the bank'	
8	Reduce the amount of information in a sentence	Make sure you speak slowly and clearly, pausing when necessary to check comprehension	
9	Use simple words	The word 'danger' (danger is a concept, an idea) can be harder for someone to understand than words like 'bicycle' or 'sandwich' (these are actual physical things)	
10	Use positives rather than negatives whenever possible	Say 'do you want to go swimming?' instead of 'what we could do, but only if you fancy it, is go swimming'	

- whether or not the communication culture of the setting values and respects the methods of communication you use to support the individual's understanding.

As a communication partner, it is **your responsibility** to modify your verbal communication. Responsibility does **not** lie with the person you are supporting.

As a communication partner, when you modify your verbal communication you support the individual's comprehension, and therefore also their expression.

Listening to facial expressions, body language and behaviour

When listening to facial expressions, body language and behaviour, it is a good idea to think of yourself as a 'communication detective'. Observation is key here and it is important that you identify and respond to all behaviours as forms of communication. The golden rule is to follow the individual's lead.

You should be able to tell whether the person you are supporting is calm or agitated by the way they are behaving. If the person is calm, for example, they may:

- sit down
- have relaxed facial expressions
- make eye contact
- turn towards you
- sign to you that they are happy
- engage in peaceful activities or those that you know they enjoy.

If someone is agitated or upset they may:

- become louder or start exhibiting distressed behaviour
- avoid eye contact
- engage in stereotyped behaviours such as head banging
- engage in self-injurious behaviour
- move around a lot and refuse to stay still.

Eye gaze

We all use eye gaze to communicate, although people without additional needs are often not aware that they are doing so. Eye gaze can be a vital form of communication for people who are non-verbal and who rely on their body language to communicate.

'Listening' to eye gaze means at all times being aware and observant of the individual you are supporting so as not to miss any invitation to communicate. Eye gaze is an effective way of communicating when the individual has an observant and responsive communication partner. It can be used to support what you are saying to the individual by looking at an object or place, or drawing the individual's attention to it.

Eye gaze can be used to determine what the person wants or what is bothering them, by the communication partner following their gaze. Eye gaze can also allow the person to exercise choice – the communication partner follows the person's gaze when they are being given a choice between a limited range of options, these perhaps being represented by pictures or objects held up in front of them.

Case study: George

George lacks verbal skills and communicates mainly with eye gaze. However, his eye gaze can be quite subtle. In order to communicate with him, his support worker, Peter, needs to be engaged and to show an interest in George, and has to be observant in order to understand what George wants to communicate.

One morning, Peter has observed George and understood that he wants to talk about either the DVD he is watching, represented by the DVD player, or his family, represented by a photo of his family on the wall. In order to determine which, Peter uses his hands to represent each choice and then observes which hand George focuses his gaze on. This technique is called distinguishing hands. Alternatively, Peter might have used the DVD case and the photo of George's family.

Gesture

Like eye gaze, we all use gesture but, again, people without additional needs are often not aware that they are doing so. By using natural gesture as you talk, you can support an individual's understanding of what you are saying.

Just as someone might use eye gaze to communicate a choice or express a wish, so too might someone use gesture by pointing or nodding.

Together or separately, eye gaze and gesture are valuable ways of communicating and can aid understanding between a support worker and the person they are supporting.

Remember the EPIC model of communication – when you are thinking about the use of eye gaze and gesture, always consider:

Thinking activity

What do you think might be the main challenges in supporting someone who uses eye gaze to communicate?

- the impact of the communication environment (is the setting too bright? Are there too many distractions?)
- your own use of and response to eye gaze and gesture
- the individual's use of eye gaze and gesture
- whether the communication culture of the setting where the individual is being supported values and respects eye gaze and gesture as valid means of communication.

Thinking activity

Think of the people you support. Does anyone use eye gaze or gesture to communicate?

Objects for communication

Objects are often used as a means of communication with people who have learning disabilities.

Objects can be used in two ways:

1. Comprehension: showing an individual a relevant object can support their understanding of what is going to happen (for example, a mug to represent having a cup of tea).

2. Expression: the individual can use objects as a means of requesting something, rejecting something, making choices or expressing preferences (for example, using their swimming costume to express a desire to go to the swimming pool).

The benefits of using objects to communicate are that they physically represent the activity or place in question, and they are easier to understand for some individuals than pictures.

However, objects for communication also present some challenges – they can be mislaid, for example, or they may not be to hand when an individual needs them. Furthermore, a communication partner may not know about the individual's way of using objects for reference and so not respond to invitations to communicate when they are made. Again, this shows the importance of getting to know the person you are supporting and finding out about their particular communication skills and preferences.

For these reasons, it is also important to have a range of techniques available for communication, should it prove difficult or not possible to use a particular technique at any given time. This is why a Total Communication approach is so important as a means of optimising communication.

Signing

Different signing systems are often used as a means of communication with people who have learning

Write down two objects that could be used to signify each of the following:

Going on a trip in the car:

1.

2.

Personal care:

1.

2.

Going swimming:

1.

2.

That it's time to eat:

1.

2.

That it's time to go to sleep:

1.

2.

disabilities. Signing can be used with individuals who are non-verbal as well as with those who are verbal as the different signs look like what they represent, providing the individual with more information than a verbal message alone.

For many individuals, signing is an important means of communication which can support them to become more verbally expressive. Key word signing by the communication partner can also support an individual's comprehension – it not only draws their attention to the key words but also naturally slows down the speech

Thinking activity

What might be some of the barriers to using signing to communicate? How would you go about overcoming these barriers?

of the communication partner and encourages them to consider their word choices.

Often people will not sign unless they are signed to. It is the responsibility of the communication partner to support the individual's use of signing. In rich signing environments, more staff sign and so more individuals sign.

Thinking activity

Why are pictures, photographs and symbols so important for communication when using a Total Communication approach?

Pictures, photographs and symbols

Like objects and signing, pictures, photographs and symbols can be used to support the individual's expression and comprehension.

- Expression: pictures, photographs and symbols are versatile and can be used in a variety of communication aids, supporting people to make positive choices, express emotions, to say 'no', to share personal experiences and to introduce ideas.

- Comprehension: pictures, photographs and symbols are concrete and permanent. They serve to focus the individual's attention on what's being talking about, drawing the individual's attention to the key words.

Pictures, photographs and symbols are motivating and can represent an almost limitless range of ideas, objects and activities. They are light and portable and can be put to a wide variety of uses and, in pictures or photographs, the individual themselves can be included.

In a sequence strip, a series of pictures or photographs can be used to help break down and explain a new skill, such as making a cup of tea, or for explaining a planned sequence of activities, such as going on the bus and then for a swim followed by a cup of tea in the cafe.

| shower | wash hair | dry yourself | put pyjamas on |

Pictures, photographs and symbols can also be used to support those who communicate through eye gaze or gesture by, for example, providing a visual representation of a selection of options from which the person can use eye gaze or gesture to choose.

Picture diaries can be used to keep a record of what an individual has been up to, which in turn can serve as a useful prompt for support workers or family members to initiate conversation or interaction.

Communication passports and multimedia profiles

Communication passports

A communication passport is essentially a book or folder that contains all the information about an individual that they want or would want you to know so that this information is easily transferred between people and settings. A communication passport can provide critical information for new staff, relief staff and hospital staff

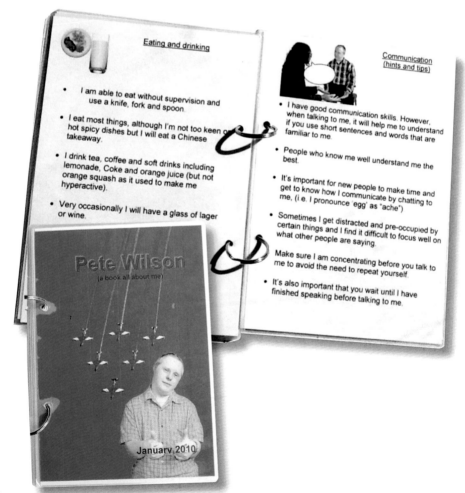

Eating and drinking

- I am able to eat without supervision and use a knife, fork and spoon.
- I eat most things, although I'm not too keen on hot spicy dishes but I will eat a Chinese takeaway.
- I drink tea, coffee and soft drinks including lemonade, Coke and orange juice (but not orange squash as it used to make me hyperactive).
- Very occasionally I will have a glass of lager or wine.

Communication (hints and tips)

- I have good communication skills. However, when talking to me, it will help me to understand if you use short sentences and words that are familiar to me.
- People who know me well understand me the best.
- It's important for new people to make time and get to know how I communicate by chatting to me, (i.e. I pronounce 'egg' as "ache")
- Sometimes I get distracted and pre-occupied by certain things and I find it difficult to focus well on what other people are saying.

Make sure I am concentrating before you talk to me to avoid the need to repeat yourself.

- It's also important that you wait until I have finished speaking before talking to me.

Pete Wilson
(a book all about me)

January 2010

when an individual is away from their usual care setting. In addition, a communication passport can be used by the individual to make requests or to initiate conversations, both practical and social.

A communication passport should include information on topics such as:

- the person's likes and dislikes eg. people, food, drink, hobbies, daily routines, outings, clothes, colours
- their preferred means of communication
- the kind of communication environment they prefer
- their family and friends
- what the person can do for themselves and what they may need support with
- information about their physical and mental health and any medication.

Communication passports can contain written information, photographs, pictures – anything that conveys the requisite information to the reader.

It is important that the individual is able to access their own communication passport so that it can be used as an effective tool for two-way communication.

Remember, a communication passport is a working document and should be kept up to date to reflect the individual's changing capacities and circumstances.

Multimedia profiles

Multimedia profiles are similar to communication passports and can

Thinking activity

What would you like others to know about you if you were to wake up tomorrow no longer able to communicate verbally?

be used particularly effectively with people with profound and multiple learning disabilities. They comprise a number of short, simple film clips that capture essential information about the individual, their communication abilities and other needs and preferences. Multimedia profiles can be stored on an iPad, laptop computer or on a DVD or memory stick and should, like communication passports, be kept up to date to reflect the individual's changing capacities and circumstances.

A multimedia profile can be used to capture sometimes very subtle communication behaviours that might otherwise be missed, and for this reason it is a powerful communication aid.

People with learning disabilities benefit greatly from having a communication passport or multimedia profile. However, there is no point in their having one if it is left at home or just stays in their bag. It is up to the communication partner to support the individual to use their passport or profile by asking if or making sure that they have it with them, using it to initiate conversations, making sure it is used regularly in the person's day-to-day life and ensuring it is kept up to date.

Visual timetables

Many people with learning disabilities have difficulty understanding concepts of time. Visual timetables are essentially a form of diary, allowing the person to keep track of upcoming events in a way that is easy for them to understand. While some individuals may have a good understanding of what is happening on a particular day, they may struggle to understand what is happening over the rest of the week. For others, not knowing what is happening over the course of a day or week can be a cause of anxiety.

A visual timetable can significantly reduce this anxiety, and this in turn can have a positive effect on the individual's communication, receptively as well as expressively. A visual timetable is easy to create and can make a big difference to a person's lived experience.

Visual timetables usually take the form of a series of photos, pictures or symbols, often including a picture of the individual themselves, stuck up on a strip of cardboard with Velcro. These photos, pictures and symbols represent the sequence of events planned for that day or week. A visual timetable might be broken down into morning, afternoon and evening, or perhaps the days of the week, depending on the person you are supporting and what is most appropriate for them.

After an activity is over, the individual is encouraged to go to the visual timetable and remove the picture representing that activity, helping the individual to understand that that activity is now finished.

Remember the EPIC model of communication – when you are thinking about the use of visual timetables, always consider:

- the impact of the communication environment (eg. are individuals supported to have a visual timetable? Are they supported to use it effectively?)

- your own use of visual timetables with the people you support (eg. is their visual timetable easily accessible? Do you support the person to remove the picture once an activity is finished?)

- the individual's use of their visual timetable (how often do they use their visual timetable? Is it a useful resource for them?)

Thinking activity

In what ways do you think a visual timetable can contribute towards increasing an individual's self-confidence?

- whether or not the communication culture of the setting where the individual is being supported values and respects the use of visual timetables as a form of communication. Do all those who support the individual know about, and know how to use, their visual timetable?

Thinking activity

Considering the advantages and disadvantages of hi-tech communication aids, do you think there will always be a role for other, more 'low-tech aids' such as visual timetables or gesture, and if so, why?

Hi-tech communication aids

There are a range of hi-tech communication aids available to support people with learning disabilities, some more hi-tech than others. Voice output devices, for example, might be a simple button that the individual presses to play a pre-recorded message. At the other end of the scale, a laptop computer or tablet computer such as an iPad enables the person to type in whatever they want to express and then audibly transmits the person's selected symbols or written words through a speaker.

More and more such devices are now becoming available relatively cheaply, and you can download a number of applications for tablets and smart phones that can have a positive or even transformative impact on the lives of the people you support. For example, there are autism timers that can be downloaded and used to support the person to understand when an activity will start or finish, as well as downloadable symbols packages which can be readily used to create a visual timetable. Similarly, photos can be taken on the tablet and incorporated directly into a visual timetable or visual diary that you are creating.

Tablets and smart phones have a number of advantages:

- They often use voice output, so anyone who understands speech can use them.

- Communication partners do not need to learn a new skill.

- They can make it possible for the person to access other activities such as using the telephone or Skype or being able to control their environment, for example by opening and closing the curtains and turning the lights, television or radio on and off.

- They do not carry the stigma of being a communication aid.

- They are lightweight.

- They can be used with other accessories to make them more accessible.

- They are getting smaller with larger memories.

- New software is available relatively cheaply.

There are, however, also some disadvantages:

- Their batteries can run out or there may be nowhere to plug them in.
- They can break or malfunction.
- They can be difficult to use in certain environments, such as in the rain or if there is no flat surface to rest the device on.

Remember the EPIC model of communication – when you are thinking about the use of hi-tech communication aids, always consider:

- the impact of the communication environment:
  - Is the device's volume loud enough to be heard?
  - Does the individual need a table to rest the device on?
  - If you are outside, does the device have a cover so it doesn't get wet?
- your own role in supporting someone in using a hi-tech communication aid:
  - Do you allow the individual enough typing time as well as processing time?
  - Have you made sure that the device is in working order and that the batteries are charged?
  - Have you made sure the person has a lo-tech alternative communication aid available in case of technical difficulties?
- the individual's use of their hi-tech communication aid:
  - Is the individual's device the most appropriate one for their needs and abilities?
  - If the individual starts to feel tired, does this affect their ability to use the device effectively?
- whether or not the communication culture of the setting where the individual is being supported values and respects the use of hi-tech communication aids as a form of communication.

Resources

The Challenging Behaviour Foundation has an informative information sheet on communication and challenging behaviour: http://www.challengingbehaviour.org.uk/learning-disability-files/03_Communication.pdf

Mencap has a useful guide to communicating with people with profound and multiple learning disabilities at: http://www.mencap.org.uk/sites/default/files/documents/2009-02/2008.292%20Mencap_Guide_Communicating_with_PMLD.pdf

Mencap has also produced a report entitled *Communication and People With the Most Complex Needs: What works and why this is essential*, which can be found at: http://www.mencap.org.uk/sites/default/files/documents/2010-12/Comms_guide_dec_10.pdf

The British Institute of Learning Disabilities (BILD) has a number of useful resources:

- a factsheet on communication: http://www.bild.org.uk/EasySiteWeb/GatewayLink.aspx?alId=2517
- a short introduction to communication as a human right: http://www.bild.org.uk/our-services/books/communication-is-a-human-right/communication-is-a-human-right/
- a learner workbook, *Communicating Effectively with People with a Learning Disability*, designed to support the Level 2 and 3 Diplomas in Health and Social Care (learning disability pathway) and the Common Induction Standards: http://www.bild.org.uk/our-services/books/communication-is-a-human-right/communicating-effectively-with-people/

Mencap and BILD have co-produced a comprehensive practical guide called Involve Me, which is about involving people with profound and multiple learning disabilities in decision-making and consultation. It can be downloaded from: http://www.bild.org.uk/about-bild/ourwork/involve-me/

COMMUNICATION for PERSON CENTRED PLANNING, produced by the Foundation for People with Learning Disabilities, is an information pack designed to help staff, self advocates, families and friends to make communication better. The aim is to help people to better understand the communication styles of self-advocates: http://www.learningdisabilities.org.uk/content/assets/pdf/publications/communication_p_c_planning.pdf

The RCSLT have produced a document called 'Five good communication standards' which sets out the reasonable adjustments to communication that individuals with learning disability and/or autism should expect in specialist hospital and residential settings: http://www.rcslt.org/news/docs/good_comm_standards

- The Communication Bill of Rights: http://www.oxtc.co.uk/resources/Communication%20Bill%20of%20Rights.pdf
- Photosymbols is a company which offers a range of symbols and images able to be used in place of or alongside text to convey a message: http://www.photosymbols.com/
- A useful total communication resource pack produced by East Sussex Total Communication: http://www.eastsussex.gov.uk/NR/rdonlyres/8E4D6DA3-4C6A-4D4F-9B67-5884AAC7184C/0/TotalCommunicationResourcePackopt.pdf

Three useful websites on total communication:

- http://www.oxtc.co.uk/
- http://www.totalcommunication.org.uk/
- http://www.totalcommunication.uk.com/

For Intensive Interaction, the following two DVDs from Phoebe Caldwell are indispensable:
Creative Conversations: http://www.pavpub.com/creative-conversations/
Learning the Language: http://www.pavpub.com/learning-the-language/

Notes